THE
EXORCISM

CATASTROPHIC

THE EXORCISM

iUniverse books may be ordered through booksellers or by contacting:

iUniverse
1663 Liberty Drive
Bloomington, IN 47403
www.iuniverse.com
844-349-9409

ISBN: 978-1-6632-2558-0 (sc)
ISBN: 978-1-6632-2559-7 (hc)
ISBN: 978-1-6632-2557-3 (e)

Library of Congress Control Number: 2021913284

Print information available on the last page.

iUniverse rev. date: 06/30/2021

CYBER—VIRUS

Social media was designed for us to reach out to peers,
And somehow it has led to steering them into headlights like a lost deer.
"See this body? This is how you're supposed to be,
Not round like a cookie.
And you have to live your life like Snookie."
Why do we always feel like we have to be everything we're not?
What if we're actually really hot?
But since we don't have a six-pack or big muscles, we're automatically not.
One thought that I've had that's making me mad is that
You never see male body-positivity posts. and it doesn't seem to make
anyone else sad.
I've been judged for my looks,
And I'll go back to that later in this book.
Another thing about the media is that I remember when I was younger,
This random lady sent me a message saying that she wanted to satisfy
my "hunger."
But all you ever see nowadays
Are the people who try to portray men as the only reason for a bad day.
Are we supposed to just keep this on the low?
I feel like this is a low blow
To Ms. Ginsburg, who fought for feminism,
Because that's the idea in which you stand with him.
"Stop sexualizing woman! It's not appropriate," and I agree.
But if a boy liked a photo with a girl in a bikini,
He's called an L7 weenie.
He could've liked it due to the flow of her hair.

And some of you people don't actually care
To listen to the real reason.
You just think that he's creepin'.
People assuming why he liked this picture
Has me in a mixture.
Shouldn't this qualify as sexism?
A girl liked that same photo but apparently disgusting behavior only
exists within him.
These folks are just casting a spell, like Gargamell.
You know, I'm all about love, and they turn it around and make me
look E-V-O-L.
"Uhh, typo?" No
Evil is love spelt backward.
I also don't get the rules of the game
That the media plays.
The odds are never in my favor.
If I don't post or share something against sex trafficking,
It apparently means that I'm just sitting back and laughing.
I'm not against the movement at all.
But there have been people saying that I should fall
Because I didn't post what they did.
I will always love and care for a kid.
And again, what's up with this, "Keep your kids away from random men"?
What about random women?
We can't trust them either.
This cold belief has made people sick in the head, like a fever.
There was even a time where someone didn't get what I said.
"You're invalidating people's opinions," uhh … what?
Did you just pull that crap out of your butt?

This isn't intended to put anyone in a rut.

I just don't understand why these people only see my gender as a threat.

Women aren't perfect either; get that in your head.

I truly don't want us to be fighting; I just want us to make this place better.

Let's just come together.

Speaking of unity, hating on white folks won't get rid of the ghost of the past.

Racism was the first thing this country saw, and if we're not careful, it'll be the last.

People have been saying Eminem doesn't belong in rap because he isn't black.

That's like saying Larry Bird shouldn't fly to the rim because he's white.

Do you see why this isn't right?

Some other stuff to mention about sports is the treatment that the Raiders get daily.

They get fined for not wearing masks, but if you see the Bucs and Brady

Without one, just ignore it.

The NFL won't even deplore it.

We need to make Goodell like the penalty calls, get him out of control.

It's not just me who feels this way; go look at the poll.

Also, Good Morning Football loves to screw over Vegas.

They don't care how angry they make us.

They're just passing out crap like an anus.

They disregard the truth from their booths, and they discuss that Crabtree

Wanted to fight Talib.

Everyone loves to throw the Raiders in the dirt,

And they never find it absurd.

Herbert gets his helmet scraped, and the flags go insane,

While Renfrow got his helmet deflated, and the officials just looked the other way.

Josh Jacobs apparently used his helmet as a weapon; if he was on another team, they

Wouldn't have worded it this way.

And you guys think this is okay?

The morning crew also loves to scrap Carr for defensive errors.

I don't know how this is fair.

Kyle Brandt goes on a rant and tells Derek to do something about it.

Then when the Raiders beat the Chiefs,

He's all of a sudden opening up his love for DC.

Another note that I have about the sports media

Is that Skip Bayless is tripping like Expedia.

Dak Prescott opens up about his battle with mental health,

And Bayless tells him to quit the yelp

And to get back on the field to help.

His team, I don't understand how a man could be so harsh

Toward another man who's falling apart.

Some other stuff that's in the dark

Is the fact in which people can catch a pass from Brady with one hand,

But it only happened because Brady is "the man."

Same thing with Lebron.

They only focus on him, regardless of what team he's on.

Don't get me wrong,

They're good players, so I'm not trying to lower their grade.

But commentators and sports analysists say the team wins because of the great

Players that they are.

But their teams are the reasons they got that far.

Imagine getting the credit for the win, but the blame for a loss goes to the teammates.

I never see them deflect that disrespect; so much for being a good teammate.

Also, why can't people leave Miss Billie Eilish alone?

She's always working hard; she's in the zone.

But these critics want to go

And criticize her for wearing a tank top.

When does the criticism from the critters stop?

Like the ones who view me as a thug only because I'm a Dodger fan.

Let me tell you something you probably won't want to understand.

Just like with color or gender, we're not all the same.

I didn't start that flame, so don't state my name.

Speaking of flame, I think it's time we tame

The crap remarks regarding mental health.

People reach out for help, and they're told not to yelp

Because they're just a complainer.

But you can cry that a mom breastfeeds her baby in public; do me a favor,

And save your comments for later.

Especially those of you who tell me to keep my parental guidance to myself.

You don't like to listen to anyone else,

Even if they have good words to share.

Yeah, I'm not a dad yet, but I still care

That you left your baby in the car seat.

No one, let alone a child, can put up with the heat.

I also know that the older generations look down on us.

They're supposed to be mentors, but there's an imposter among us.

"Get off your phones! Communicate with your peers.

Excuse me dear,

Can you help me fix the wee fee?"

But back to what I was saying,

The media is filled with stuff that I will continue to break down like a detox pill.

Or should I say like Knox Hill?

Anyway, I know people will try to give me critiques on my writing

While despising my message that I'm displaying in the lighting.

My grammar may be off from time to time,

But if mumbling rappers can blow up by saying the same word to rhyme in every line,

I can for sure make a dime with the lines that I design in my mind.

I also don't know why

It's okay for anyone to send death threats to any human being.

They're imperfect, just like you, but only if you care to see.

I also understand if you disagree

With what they said, but to go for their heads in that way is not okay.

Again, disagree with what they say.

Sending threats is not okay.

To end my donkey-of-the-day speech,

I love this world, and I want it to be better, which is why I try to align

Words that'll put us in a straight line

To a greater future; I'll stick my hand out if you need me.

I just want you to promise me you'll stand beside me

So we can both be knights like Stevie.

You figure out what to pursue in your life,

And I finally meet my wife.

With that being said, I feel like we need

To do better in saying that everyone has a purpose.

Those feelings need to be a surplus.

I don't want anyone to feel alone, as I do.

To anyone who feels this way, I stand beside you

Because at the end of the day, I'm human just like you.

Oh yeah, for those of you who use anyone's medical condition as a way

to build your likes, you disgust me.

BLASPHEMY

My folks raised me to be a gentleman.
I was able to form myself into medicine
So I can heal others, and I know I had a rough start.
I was a kid, and to understand love was hard.
These days I'm apparently too soft and too sweet.
I've seen that some women want men to sweep
Them off of their feet.
But nowadays proper manners are perceived
As cheesy lines.
It doesn't even matter how hard I try to be nice,
I have to be spicy
In order for a woman to like me.
How would you even know if that's true?
I wouldn't even know what to do.
I admire woman; I can't be rude
To someone whom I'm trying to move
Into my arms and heart.
To me that's not a good start.
Not to mention
Some hearts are in tension
Because someone's intentions
Were to play a game and drive the lady insane
So her brain won't remain the same
Ever again.
She wants pain to end.
How can you blame her?

Another thing that cuts away at my gut

Is that America gave this guy clout

For talking about

His past.

They won't even let me take off my cast

To see how much healing I've done.

People say that they wish they would have noticed,

But they didn't care to notice

My diagnosis

On why my rose is

Losing its petals.

I'm feeling heavy, like some metal.

I wish for these knots to become untangled,

So I can be there for my kid without being strangled.

TO WHOM IT MAY CONCERN

There are children who like school,

And that's cool.

But I don't,

They're awake, but I'm woke.

Since kindergarten I've been nothing but a joke.

That's probably why the kids laughed at me.

School has blasted me with this blasphemy

That I need college

So I avoid a stigma and keep my knowledge.

Little do they know my heart needs polish

The way a kid needs a ball pit.

This is your word problem; go ahead and solve it.

You contain more bull crap than a bull.

Why don't you just eat it till you're full?

Oh, I'm sorry, am I being rude?

Do my words contain cruelty?

School was cruel to me

Because when I fight back, I'm the bully.

You know what? Go ahead and sue me.

But you can't shush me.

"Miss, Taylor Andrew pushed me."

"Shut your trap! You did it first."

"Hey, don't curse."

"Two wrongs don't make a right."

That doesn't make sense to me in the slightest

Because when she did it, it was okay.

I feel like I should've stayed home and acted like it was a snow day
So I wouldn't feel like exploding. as if I'm a tank filled with propane.
School is like the Holocaust; I got gassed out. Look at the strength
Those halls have cost me.
There are scars and bruises all across me.
I must be a salad since school tossed me
Around in a bowl of doubts and insecurities.
I need help, but I have no special needs,
So no one will help me see the B on my test sheet.
You know what? Fine, don't help me.
Since I don't have ADHD,
My conflicts don't exist.
School's overall attention to me showed up like an eclipse—
Unless there was something I missed.
Here is another question I have on my list.
Why is it that the school's attention only goes to the A?
You don't know the journey I took to get to where I am today.
I had a challenging quest; I have value you shouldn't degrade.
My flowers are just as beautiful, but since my skies are gray,
You only acknowledge the rain.
It also told me that I can be anything I set my mind to.
But what I wanted to do didn't involve what you
Wanted me to be or achieve.
So at what point do you just leave?
This issue needs to be solved
Before it becomes dissolved,
And we can no longer see it.
School grades you based on the other kids' ability.
Is it just me, or is that silly?

Also, I don't have the ability to walk, so don't ask me to run. "But why?"

It's something I can't do even if I tried.

School is a place to cry and die.

All they want is your money; they don't even care if you're alive.

There was a time when the teacher didn't care that I asked for help.

She'd rather have me yelp

To my classmates,

But they would just get aggravated

That I stated

A word; I must be a turd since they flushed me away.

When I needed your guidance,

You told me that I never tried it.

Tried what? To ask a question?

I did! Go back and reread this message.

This is why you'll never see me as a student again.

DEAR MEAN GIRLS

Love is a very important part of life.

That's why we need to pass it around like a slice.

But some people would rather use it as a knife

To cut through a dude

Who did nothing to you.

"Men are trash,"

Is an idea that's straight ass.

Some are bad, but I still hear that we should kill all men.

I've been mistreated by girls since I was ten.

My heart went for a whirl,

And I never once wanted to kill a girl.

These crap ideas have me filled with so much vengeance

That I'm beginning to feel like a sith apprentice.

There was a girl at my school who said, "Men are terrible,"

And that thought alone should be unbearable.

Apparently the guys who were acceptable were too ugly to be with.

I was just a frog wanting a princess to kiss.

Was I poorly treated because you thought I would destroy your ego?

Well it's too late now. Down memory lane is where we go.

Don't you just love being treated like mice?

I understand if you have a type, but that doesn't make it right

To shame the ones you don't want. Do you not have class?

Women shouldn't have to clean, but clean up your act.

I know I'm being anal, but to you guys I've always been a pain in the ass.

Back in school you treated me like an unpleasant peasant

Who had an unwanted presence.

Even the ones who were friendly

And supported me ran from me.

I have a wild life; I'm on the channel of discovery.

That's where they discovered me.

Nowadays I just want to be respected, not asking for you to treasure me.

Speaking of treasury,

I never had enough luxury, not just money, but because my appeal wasn't ideal.

It's not really a highlight, but it's on my reel.

That the "cool kids" wanted to make me feel,

Like I wasn't enough

To be her love.

Being with this girl should have been impossible

Because she's a three-course meal, and I'm a Lunchable.

One of my female friends tried to imply on the way to school

That she thought I was a fool

Since I wasn't able to see that her and me

Shouldn't have been a possibility.

Then later in the year, when I found someone else to love,

People wanted to say, "Congrats"

Even though they're all rats.

I never gave anyone crap, even when I thought they were lame.

I stayed in my lane, and never said their names.

There are guys like me who get shamed since we're not six foot four.

Some ladies are craving relations, and I never call them a … you know what.

Some may still laugh at me for being a virgin because apparently sex is a milestone.

Love is not about making anyone moan.

It's to unite and make sure your other half doesn't feel alone.

I'm surprised you guys didn't know that considering you're full grown.

Now you know why all this men crap keeps me heated like foil.

My heart is ice, and my mind is boiled.

Sorry that I wasn't pretty.

That didn't mean I couldn't treat you right from now to infinity.

"Never body shame a woman."

Whoa, man.

I was told stuff like, "Ew, no, get away. You're fat.

I prefer my men to be like Chris Pratt

Or even Chris Hemsworth."

And because of that, I wasn't worth

Your time, even though I

Would've treated you fine.

One time a girl called me a mistake

Because my face wasn't right, and it should have never been placed

Next to the girl I was with.

Even my teacher's words were a stitch.

This has made me a despicable individual

And left me feeling like my beauty was mythical.

Lately there have been a lot of ladies saying that feel like men hate them,

And I could definitely say the same about women.

Love should have never been toxic.

Sincerely,
Catastrophic

A Quiet Place

I hope to be a good father.
I'm in fear of having a misguided daughter.
I wish for her to follow what I taught her,
But seeing the kids I grew up with, I know that my teachings could falter.
She can grow taller,
But her brain can obtain and sustain the containment of discombobulation.
All I ask of her is to find a nonsexual occupation.
If that's all she sees, I didn't do my part.
I failed to fill her heart
With not only knowledge but wisdom.
There are points that I'm targeting, and I don't want to miss them.
I know I need to keep her in check,
But I don't want to leave her heart wrecked.
Needing to physically discipline my child leaves me haunted
Because I need to parent, but that's not how I want it.
The moment I make my daughter cry
Is the moment where I fully die inside.
Just think of you trying to lie down on a Temperpedic,
And her temper is repeatedly
Rising at every hour.
I'm sorry, sweetie, if I ever make you feel sour.
I also hope to be a good spouse.
I'll do what I can around the house
I'll help clean, and I'll help to place food on our plates.

I can't be controlling, so I'll give her space.

And that means I can't keep people from touching her face.

I hope to marry a woman with good morals.

In other words, I don't want her love to be mortal.

I don't know why I fear being cheated on; I can only do my part by giving her love,

And I just hope that I'm good enough.

I broke down the bacteria

That's giving me this hysteria

In mean girls.

My head is in a whirl.

They chose the guys who are built like Michael B. Jordan.

This insecurity went straight to storage.

Now I'm peeling like an orange.

Sometimes it hits me while I'm eating porridge.

These are the emotions I'm pouring out at the gym.

That's how I'm feeling within.

Nowadays there's a lot about woman being mistreated,

And when I want to mention my life, I'm told to beat it.

We love to learn about the past because that's our path,

But we refuse to listen to the news about his story.

I admire women, so I gave compliments and a toast,

And I keep getting treated like a joke.

You can clearly see that we have the same battles.

So then why do you leave me rattled?

Both of our hearts are fragile,

But you only want yours to be handled

With care.

Thanks for being there

For me and the other men on the street.
These are the feels that I keep deep down,
This is what causes a frown every now
And again.
I just want this pain to end.
Maybe I need a true, genuine girl friend,
One who won't hurt me for not being a ten.
And one who doesn't hate men.
My guy friends treat me splendidly.
It's just that a lady friend has different chemistry.

THE COMPLAINER

My mental health isn't treated.

When I speak on it, I get told to beat it.

It feels like I'm getting cleated.

This makes me so heated.

I have a lot to say, so get seated.

I tell you I need help. and you don't believe it.

You think I'm being deceiving.

When I say I'm tempted to leave, your irritability hits the ceiling.

Why don't you care about how I'm feeling?

My skin is thick, but it's peeling

Like an orange.

There's no room in my self-storage.

In the morning I hardly eat my porridge.

"There are kids with no food.

And you're just being rude

If you don't empty that bowl."

My head isn't in the zone.

I'm feeling alone.

"There are homeless out in the cold.

There are parents who can't raise their own

Children in a good environment.

People are struggling to save money for retirement."

Anger is about to explode like water from a hydrant.

"You know there are people with no legs.

Go ahead and tell me about your bad day."

That's what they say when they want us to go away.

It's always in an antagonizing way.

I'm not trying to be your highness.

I just want to be treated with kindness.

I start to speak about feeling weak,

And then my words get tweaked:

"You're alive, so just live."

I can't with demons within.

Have you ever had these thoughts,

The ones that make your heart rot,

The ones that leave you in a tough spot?

I bet you have no idea,

Yet you keep laughing like a hyena

I don't fear death; I fear the life I may not have.

I attempt to be glad,

And then I get hit with a pain you don't understand.

Yeah, I cry, and I'm still a man

With a plan to expand

My family

And to me, that's like winning a Grammy.

My agony isn't comical, like Stan Lee.

You're probably confused to see me

Having fun out in the sun.

But in the dark it's hard to speak since I always have to bite my tongue.

Try breathing when your emotions are squeezing your lungs.

I'm no longer giving my loyalty to one who treats me as spoiled beans.

Throwing me away doesn't deserve royalty.

"Is your cup half full or half empty? Doesn't matter. Drink the water."

I'd rather save it for my daughter

Because I'm going to be a loving father.

That's why I'm here.

I fight through every tear, so I can help her grow strong year after year.

And I want to be near so when she cries, she is able to hear me in her ear.

I'll preach strength in things where I had fear.

We all have burning love, like Elvis.

Also, aren't suicidal people considered selfish?

"Why did he kill himself?

He didn't stop to think about how my hearts would've melted.

He didn't even go through that much shit; it was just a pellet.

I mean he seemed okay. He smiled and laughed."

We all try to fly high like a kite in the sky, but we're at half-staff.

"I feel like I lost my better half."

That sucks for you.

Do those words sound hateful? Doesn't matter; you have a plateful,

Just be grateful.

"Hey bro, I miss you."

Sounds like a personal issue.

"He should've spoken up."

No worries; you still have half the cup.

There is no intent to say your life is easier than mine is.

I'm tired of mental illnesses being degraded like a minus.

Why is it that I can't discuss the illness within my head,

But Karen gets to speak to a manager that her toast tastes like bread?

Opposites Aren't Attracting

(Intermission)

You tell me to practice what I preach,

But no one else seems to learn from what they teach.

You say I need to be respectful,

But your actions toward me are neglectful.

Since the youth I've been held to a different standard.

Everyone has been trying to hunt me like a mallard.

You say I'm handsome,

But when it comes to compliments, no one wants to hand some.

You're trying to say I'm ideal,

But there's always something wrong with my appeal.

You say you love me

But for who you want me to be.

You say I'm not alone … but that's all people have made me feel.

THE MOST BEAUTIFUL

There's this one girl
Who makes my world
Spin.
Too bad I've committed so much sin
That it prevents me from meeting this exquisite angel.
My ways of self-love also have me tangled.
I adore her, but jealousy
Corrupts my insides like Hennessy.
I see her beautiful face, and tears start forming
Like dew in the morning.
Her clouds are forming
While mine are pouring
Hail, sleet, and snow.
I am happy for her, and I wish I could let her know.
But heaven is a place I'll probably never go.
In my last book I wrote about what she means to me,
And it may seem to be
About her looks.
But take another peek at the inspiration she has cooked.
She produces and acts—
I wanted to do both … facts.
I was just kicking back and relaxing,
And then I saw that she was attacking
And blowing up the world of artistry.
She's even doing it charmingly.
The singing and dancing,

Even editing the same movie she's acting

In.

How could this not inspire a kid?

It inspired me, so I got a keyboard; but creative juices weren't flowing

As well as I was hoping.

Then I went into writing and found my proper lighting.

I heard Joyner's *Will,* and that's where the deciding

Came into play

For me to talk about this marvelous saint.

If I ever met her, I'd probably faint

Or maybe even stutter like Boucher

Since I'd have no idea what to say.

If there's something she'd say to me,

I'd still fall, but I would do it gracefully.

She makes everything in life nicer.

I guess it's safe to say I kind of like her.

Another point I may be asked is if I think she'd feel the same.

I don't want to go there since those demons can't be tamed.

Ever since I made the decision

About pursuing the mission

To meet this darling,

I was starting

To transform into my prime form.

I wanted to meet the world as well as she did rather than staying in my dorm.

This was my motive to power through the storm.

There are times when I question if she's even real.

It should be impossible for someone to have that great of an appeal.

Also, I feel

Bad that she was sent down here with us.

People crash and burn on a bus.

There are people who go to into a church and cause a fuss.

I'm grateful she's here.

I just wish there was nothing for her to fear.

I'm not trying to say that she is afraid.

I just wish she could grow her flowers without the rain.

Why do I feel this so much?

I bet no one has heard of something such

As insane as what I'm saying.

Meeting her was part of my praying.

Since then I haven't been the same.

I'm sorry people have threatened you; I wish no tear would fall down your face,

And I wish I could take all your hurt away.

This is all honesty.

Her miraculous soul is so astonishing.

The sky is the limit, and she became a star.

Most beautiful, I truly adore the angel that you are.

I've wanted to be your man so bad.

Instead, I think I've become your Stan …

Damn.

THE EXORCISM

Why do I consist of venom?

Maybe it's because the higher power hasn't answered the prayers I sent him.

Or maybe it's because of my conflicting

Past, and I keep talking about the dissing.

Back in school I was called a fool for not being cool

Since I didn't do what they do.

When I tried it,

They didn't even like it.

I was never considered to be good enough.

I was everyone's duff,

Like my name was Hilary.

All these "cool kids" are using their wizardry to form misery.

I'm such a maroon, or even a buffoon

For not leaving the party as soon

As I wanted to.

People spoke to me,

But supposedly

They had better people to mingle with.

I was trying to hold myself together with a stitch.

Maybe I should've used staples.

I was hardly ever able to find a table

To sit at and kick back and relax before I had to head back to class.

The majority of the time I was told to move it.

Don't you love being excluded,

Being set aside like a side of fries?

Then there are the fake ones who try to make you feel alive,

But you just live a lie.

As soon as I left the room,

The gossip continued.

These opinions were always being spoken about me,

Not just about my personality,

But about my looks and body.

The "cool kids" are always being foul, but no one called a technicality

Till I spoke my reality

Of whom they are,

And all of a sudden, they act hard.

Even in the dugout

I was chasing a dream, and they chased clout.

That's all they were about.

"lOoK aT mE. i'Ve GoT aLl ThE gIrLs BeSiDe Me"—

Wow, your words are more striking

Than your pitches.

I really hated playing with those guys.

I even got heckled by the parents for doing the same things their kids did.

They can strike out, but if I do it, the parents grow livid.

I just don't get it.

You can diss me, but when I call you out, you say you never meant it.

"Fix your hat; it's crooked"; no, that's your eyes.

It explains why you haven't reached base all night.

"When you stole second base, you munched it."

I'm still batting seven hundred.

Would any of you readers be believers

If I told you I was teased even by a teacher?

She decided that it'd be nice to talk about my features.

These comments made me feel like I have poor appeal.

That's why I watch my meals.

My heart's pain tolerance is at maximum capacity.

Dealing with agony has formed a cavity.

Some may say I'm sad for attention,

But maybe their hearts haven't been in this much tension.

One thing they'll probably say is that I didn't have the life they did.

I was a kid trying to fit in,

And I had no one to communicate with.

Don't you get it?

You make sure the people you talk to are respected,

And they turn around and make you feel neglected.

I'm tired of not feeling accepted.

I'm being played like a poker chip.

And now I'm so over it.

THE ABSENTEE

Every time I wanted to die, you held me tight.

You said, "Don't cry. Just give it time, and in the end you'll be all right."

These words prevented me from crossing the line that made me think of suicide.

Without you at my side, I don't know how I would've made it through those nights.

I've faced the fact that you haven't bothered to see if I'm worse or better.

Whatever happened to "I'll love you forever"?

Did you just want to forget that we were together?

Am I such an embarrassment

That you had to bury me in the basement

Of your life?

I know I did some things that hurt you, and it was never my intent.

I've still spent

Long hours trying to get ahold of you.

Yeah, I did break a promise, and so did you.

Your honesty is what you promised me, and then you ghosted me like *The Conjuring*.

In case you say that you care, my mental health has dropped below the poverty line,

And I'm not doing fine.

I would say thank you for the affection, but I doubt you'd pay attention.

Like the time in middle school when we both did a crime, but you got detention

While I faced suspension; after all that neglection,

I should have known your intentions.

You were a queen I cherished, and I was the peasant that perished.

But there was still more love between us than in the city of Paris.

I guess it makes sense to say we're not friends

Because all you give me is your absence.

RELIGIOUSLY IN CONFUSION

Why punish me for not attending Mass?
There's already a stigma for not being in class.
Just because I don't go every Saturday
Or Sunday,
That doesn't mean I don't love you, Lord,
Or that I love another more.
Even if I did,
You wouldn't like it, and that's a sin.
"How so?" It's called pride.
This means I must call you mine.
If I need to pray, I must go to you
Because there's nothing you can't do.
You must feel some sort of jealousy.
That's a sin too; it's called envy.
I think of you every day,
But I can never hear a word you say.
You forgive us but still send us to hell
Since we fell
When we were supposed to stand.
I want to be in heaven, but now I'm banned.
You judge us based on how you make us.
You say I'm special; I must be a bust.
Why did you choose for your Son to die?
Apparently he was a great guy,
Yet you cut his life short.
What was that for?

For my sins?

I hope you went to confession for the guilt within.

You can be free

If you come to me.

Well just go to another individual

Since I'm just spiritual.

No proof I'm actually here.

But you better believe in it, dear.

Another thing I find funny

Is that you don't like greed, but the church asks me for money.

This religion still doesn't make any sense.

You have big churches, and people still live in tents.

Church isn't a museum; it's a hospital for the broken.

Then why am I still broken?

Shouldn't I have been fixed by now?

I have prayed every night for it, wow.

You flat out ignored me. "No I didn't. I still love you."

Must be why you took Grandpa and Bubba too.

You give blessings just to take them?

Do you enjoy what I have become,

A person of pain and wrath?

I feel bad, but I don't since my heart can't seem to outlast

This curse.

I pray for better, but it gets worse,

Not just for me and my family, but for the world.

Imagine living with people and still having lonely nights.

I have to teach myself to fly,

But I'm a penguin.

I have to sustain speed like Cameron Maybin.

If you are my strength, why do I train?

Apparently you come with my name.

But for your presence I still pray.

You don't have to leave me alone.

But when I get to the end zone,

I want the credit.

I sent you another prayer; I hope you've read it.

F*** Off

I was just sitting in my bed reminiscing
About all the times the kids were dissing
Me about who I dated or who I liked.
Why was I one who had such despite
Coming into his direction?
I don't get why they had to form this tension.
You kids wore underwear with Scooby-doo,
And you didn't hear me bashing you.
What kind of respect is this?
You disliked me but always spoke my name.
Even in the times when I thought you were lame,
I never went after you because it was a waste of time.
You had a hurt heart, so you tried to break mine.
If you wanted things to be that way, well I guess its fine.
You're not perfect, and nor am I.
You loved voicing your opinion about me, but why couldn't I speak my mind
On how I feel about your life?
Everything I've cooked had your added sass.
Just get to class and don't forget your hall pass.
You'd rather act a clown as an attempt to become a preacher.
You want followers, but you're no leader.
You all liked to call me Harry Potter and then got mad when I cursed.
Another thought that has just occurred
Is that you hated my voice but still loved my words.
I just laugh at the fact that you tried to put me in the dirt.

Yeah, from time to time I feel insecure, and I still know my worth,

And this poor treatment isn't what I deserve.

No one ever seemed to leave me alone.

You don't have to like my game, but I still reach the end zone.

You only dissed me because I'm different, but you hated when I tried to be you.

Does that make sense to you?

If so, that explains your grades in school.

All I ever wanted to do was fit in.

Now I'm glad I didn't.

When I attempted a trend, you'd shoot it and boot it.

Then try to compliment my lady as if she was Jennifer Love Hewitt.

During the science fair you dissed my house of sticks,

But it's as strong as your house of bricks.

You kids were always foul, which explains why you were never fair to me.

It took my mind and heart to mentor me to overlook the parody

Version you apparently attempted to portray of me.

Plus none of you girls wanted to pleasure me,

And that's okay, but why did you still stare at me?

If you want to, feel free to get lost like a pair of keys.

If you don't like what I said, you can try to sue me.

AMPUTATION

All this pain has taken my head way.

Now I have to find a way to stay stable.

I'm not horsing around

When I say bad thoughts are walking around

In my head.

I don't even know who listened or felt what I've said,

To sum up my diagnosis, I'm not feeling loved.

Yeah, okay, I have food and a car, but I'm still being shoved

Into a guillotine.

No one has cared about the people being mean to me.

I know that I'm not perfect, but I don't deserve it.

You know? The feeling of being deserted

Because I know I've done wrong, but I'm still a sweetheart.

I can't state exactly when this exorcism started,

But I can tell you about what has damaged my soul.

I never would have envisioned my soul growing cold,

Like the winter season.

When I want to talk about my problems, everyone starts leaving,

Or they basically tell me to deal with it.

Some people compare my life to others because I didn't have physical mischief.

I'm sick of my pain being underestimated or even degraded because the pain

That is contained in my membrane remains to sustain the strength of its strain.

I got body shamed, and it sent me into a whirl.

Apparently it's only important when it happens to a girl.

Maybe if I was one I'd actually matter.

This virus makes me even sadder.

I was judged for my looks all the time,

And the ones who were by my side were just passing by.

It comes to show that society only wants to know what the girl goes

Through.

Yeah, I'm a dude, but what about my pain? "Bruh, it's not about you."

I guess it never is.

I thought my junior year prom was going to be filled with bliss.

That night and the next morning I was completely missed.

Like the shots from the stormtroopers,

I'm not trying to cause problems like a boomer.

I just wish you guys had let me talk about this sooner.

My demons invested in my pain, and they became consumers.

It's so hard when no one cares about your flares.

So they just stare into the other direction and let you feel despair.

Even after the times you were there

For them and to help solve their

Problems, how's that fair?

For some reason, other beings can tell me what to do with myself like

a mayor.

Now I'm burning in Satan's lair.

I know my characteristics are rare,

And I'm doing well trying to give

Everyone my love's fulfillment and give them my forgiveness

For all the wrongs that have been done, so I can live with

You all, and we can be happy people.

So we can get rid of the evil

Spirits.

So when it comes to bigotry and bullying, we don't have to hear it.

I've made bad jokes, and from doing that, I've learned.

A lot of bad things have been said about me, and I feel like your back would turn

On me since it has been done before.

It has made my heart sore that everyone loves others more.

For example, in middle school, my ex hurt me every day.

One time, one time I threw her hand away,

And her friend texted me with some special words to say.

I guess society likes to have my life slowly churned,

And once I fall, they'll swoop down on my corpse like vultures.

They have that inner savage, and I'm trying to put words together like B-Rabbit.

I suffer from loneliness, and I'm looking for an aid that contains magic.

I know not everyone will like me.

The kids my age despise me.

I couldn't even go to a teacher

Because even to them I was a creature.

The worst experience I had with one was when my eighth-grade

History teacher decided to give my face a low grade.

The irritation with this and with the students saying that I need to stay

Six feet away from my girlfriend is part of the pain that I was told to keep under my cast.

I choose to remember my path for the fact that someone may need a patch.

To add to that, if I forget my past, I'll probably forget my path.

I get that the past can break you,

But what if it breaks you to place you into what makes you

A better person.

It can also help you to realize that you became the version

That you wanted to see in yourself.

And another thing is that I won't worry about you elves on the shelves;

You're watching for a reason.

It still hurts that my close folks committed treason.

I wonder what the meaning

Of family is; I stopped playing baseball,

And a quitter is all they saw.

That's another reason why I feel cut off.

I get ignored for three days after my gear was thrown all over the floor.

I don't get the purpose in why you try say you love me to the core

But still end up wishing I was more

Than what I am.

I just don't understand.

I can only give all I have.

Sorry I can't make you glad.

This is making me sad.

I'm a man with a plan to expand

Our family,

And critics are making it saddening

By saying I should wait for its happening.

This is what I want in my life—

Poetry, joy, a kid, and a wife.

I practically speak on this every time I write.

I know I'm dimmed, but this is my light.

Being suicidal makes me think

That I should sink

To save others.

Maybe this is the way to save my brothers so they can be with their mothers.

I say those words, and people show up all of a sudden.

I say I'm attempting to hang on my bedroom door, and everyone tries to run in.

I find it ironic how the bothering

Of the people take place after a conjuring.

It's too late to say, "I love you," to my face.

The person that I was is going to be placed

Six feet under, but if you change your ways,

You may see him again one day ... and he won't be the same.

Printed in the United States
by Baker & Taylor Publisher Services